First Shapes
in Buildings

Penny Ann Lane

F

FRANCES LINCOLN
CHILDREN'S BOOKS

circle

This roof has a large round opening
in the top. You can see the light streaming in
and making a huge pale circle on the wall.

How would it feel to walk about
in this building?

semi-circle

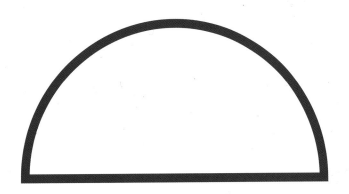

Every arch on this bridge is a semi-circle.
By joining up these arches,
the builders made a strong bridge
to cross the river.

How long do you think it would take
to walk across this bridge?

oval

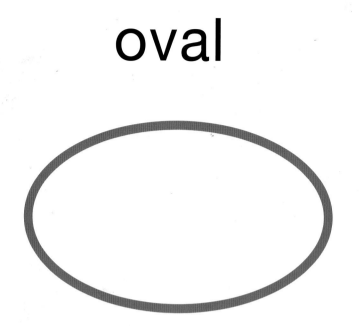

The sides of this oval piazza
look like huge arms looking after
the people inside it.

Why do you think the piazza
was built like this?

square

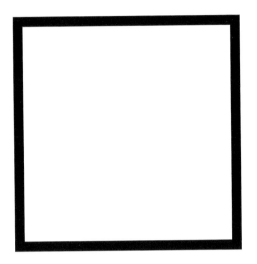

The squares in the walls of this library
look like big books!
The whole building seems to sit
on four little stones, one in each corner.

Can you see any other shapes in this picture?

rectangle

This interesting doorway is the entrance to a beautiful garden. The doors on each side make a rectangle which invites us in to look closer.

If you stepped through this doorway
what might you find?

triangle

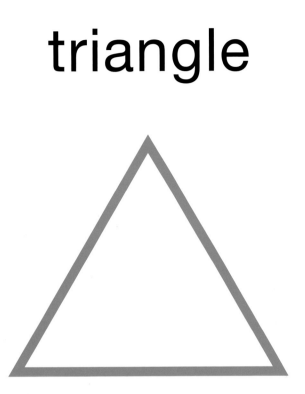

Look at the carvings of people and horses
in the triangle on the top of this building.
This picture shows everyone
the story of the people who built it.

What do you think that story might be?

sphere

The top of this sphere shines like a precious jewel.
Even from far away, everyone who sees this fabulous roof
will think of how special the space inside must be.

How would you make a roof like this?

ellipsoid

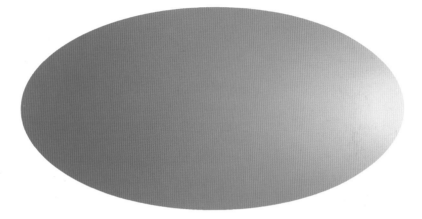

This ellipsoidal building is an office block,
though it looks more like a vegetable!
You can see glass and steel sections swirling
up the sides to the point at the top.

What do you think it would be like to go
to work in this building?

cube

This cube-like building is very important to Muslims,
who believe it was originally built by angels.
Look how the people crowd round every side.

What do you think this building is made of?

cuboid

These giant stone cuboids are part of a very old circle
of stones. Each stone was dragged many miles
and placed very carefully.

Why do you think this stone monument was built?

pyramid

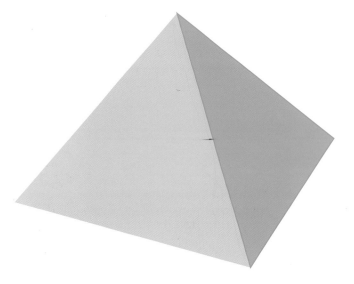

This pyramid of glass protects the people inside
from bad weather and lets light go down
into the space below.

How do people get into this space?

cylinder

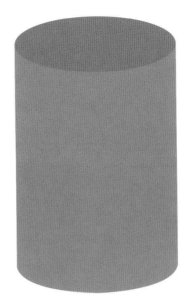

These huge cylinders look like tree trunks.
The people who built this temple believed that walking
through this forest of columns would remind them
of their journey to the next life.

How would you feel if you walked through
all these massive cylinders?

The Buildings

The Pantheon, *Rome*, Italy

Pont du Gard, *Nimes*, France

St Peter's Piazza, *Rome*, Italy

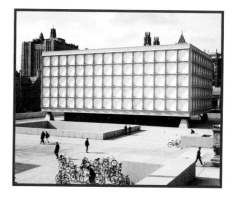

Beincke Brook Library, Yale University, *Connecticut*, USA

Imperial Villa of Katsura, *Kyoto*, Japan

The Parthenon, (artistic representation, not photo of the ruin), *Athens*, Greece

Masjid-in shah Mosque, *Isfahan,* Iran

Stonehenge, *Salisbury Plain*, UK

The Gherkin, *London*, UK

Entrance to the Louvre Museum,
Paris, France

The Ka'bah, *Makkah*, Saudi Arabia

Hypostyle Hall, Temple of Anon,
Karnak, Egypt

Photographic Acknowledgements
Please note: the pages in this book are not numbered. The text begins on page 4.

Front cover & Page 25: Exterior view of I.M. Pei's Pyramid, Louvre, Paris. Photo RMN/© Gérard Blot
Page 5: *Interior of the Pantheon, Rome*, c.1734, Giovanni Paolo Panini. Courtesy of the Board of Trustees,
National Gallery of Art, Washington (Samuel H. Kress Collection. 1939.1.24)
Page 6: Ancient Art & Architecture Collection (photo C.M. Dixon)
Page 9: © 2005. Photo Spectrum/HIP/Scala, Florence
Page 10: Photo Ezra Stoller © Esto. All rights reserved
Page 13: Photograph by Takeshi Nishikawa from *Katsura: A Princely Retreat* by Akiro Naito (Tokyo, 1977)
reproduced by kind permission of Kyoto Office of the Imperial Household, Kyoto, Japan
Page 14: Gorham P. Stevens Papers, American School of Classical Studies at Athens
Page 17: Ancient Art & Architecture Collection (photo R. Sheridan)
Page 18: Swiss Re HQ, 30 St Mary Axe, London. By courtesy of Nigel Young/Foster + Partners
Page 21: Mecca, Saudi Arabia/Bildarchiv Steffens/The Bridgeman Art Library
Page 22: Ancient Art & Architecture Collection (photo C. Hogue)
Page 26: The Art Archive/Gianni Dagli Orti

First published in Great Britain in 2009 and in the USA in 2010
by Frances Lincoln Children's Books,
4 Torriano Mews, Torriano Avenue, London NW5 2RZ
www.franceslincoln.com

British Library Cataloguing in Publication Data
available on request

ISBN 978-1-84507-695-5

Printed in China

1 3 5 7 9 8 6 4 2